Mother's Thoughts for the Day

for the Day JOURNAL

Mother's Thoughts for the Day

JOURNAL

for the Day

CREATE YOUR OWN COLLECTION OF LOVING WISDOM

Crystal Cove
PRESS®

Published by Crystal Cove Press®, Newport Beach, California
mothersthoughtsfortheday.com

Edited and designed by Girl Friday Productions
www.girlfridayproductions.com

Cover and interior design: Rachel Marek
Project management: Katherine Richards
Editorial: Tiffany Taing

ISBN (paperback): 978-1-7338657-5-3

First edition

INTRODUCTION

The Mother's Thoughts for the Day series compiles some of the best advice and encouraging words sent from my mother to me over twenty-five years.

Many readers of the series share the books with their children, reading it with them at night as they tuck them into bed or writing out some of the advice on its pages into lunch box notes for their children to discover later that day.

Readers also have expressed an interest in sharing their own advice with their children in a similar keepsake volume.

This journal provides an opportunity to do just that. It guides you in reflecting on your child's best qualities as well as your most significant hard-won advice, and combines it all into a beautiful journal to be gifted to your child.

Relax, sit back with your favorite cup of tea, and put pen to paper for your child's future.

—M.C. Sungaila

CHAPTER 1:

I Love Who You Are

YOU ARE A LOVELY PERSON AND YOU DON'T EVEN KNOW IT, AND THAT'S PART OF WHAT MAKES YOU SO SPECIAL.

As you open this journal, take a few moments to breathe and clear your mind. Now, think about your child. Reflect on how you've watched them go through different life stages, tackle new roles, and navigate tricky situations. Contemplate what you've learned by watching them explore life and how they have helped you grow.

Once you've had a chance to reflect, dive into this journal and start sharing the words in your heart. You can use the prompts on each spread or skip ahead to the final section, where free space is provided. Enjoy the journey.

If I had a daughter, I'd want her to be

just like you.

WAIT A MINUTE!! YOU ARE MY DAUGHTER. YOU *ARE* MY DAUGHTER, MY FRIEND.

I am a lucky lady.

In the space provided, compose a *personal note* to your loved one. Include at least one specific example of how your child knocks your socks off and why you feel like the LUCKIEST MOTHER OUT THERE.

_____

_____

_____

_____

_____

_____

_____

_____

_____

_____

_____

_____

_____

_____

_____

_____

_____

_____

_____

I love and
respect who
you are and
who you are
evolving into.

Reach into your memory for those FUNNY LITTLE QUIRKS your child had when they were little that hinted at their future character. (To jog your memory, look at old photos or art projects.) Share an example or two of how these traits have developed into *qualities you admire*.

_____

_____

_____

_____

_____

_____

_____

_____

_____

_____

_____

_____

_____

_____

_____

_____

_____

_____

_____

I just wanted you to know I am so in awe of you so much of the time! You just pick yourself up and push forward. You are made of the right stuff, my dear.

What are the TOP TEN WORDS that capture what's *wonderful* about your child?

1. _____

_____

2. _____

_____

3. _____

_____

4. _____

_____

5. _____

_____

6. _____

_____

7. _____

_____

8. _____

_____

9. _____

_____

10. _____

_____

_____

_____

There are people who

DO

and people who

WISH.

You are the captain of the *first.*

Think about moments when your loved one has been a person who **DOES**, and then complete the sentences below.

I was so impressed by how you . . . _____

_____

_____

_____

_____

_____

_____

_____

I WAS SO HAPPY to see you . . . _____

_____

_____

_____

_____

_____

_____

_____

You make me **SMILE** when you . . . _____

_____

_____

_____

_____

_____

_____

_____

_____

_____

_____

_____

_____

_____

_____

_____

_____

_____

_____

_____

_____

_____

I can't wait to see you . . .

Some people improve the world just by being in it.

P.S. I THINK YOU FALL IN THIS SLOT.

Create a set of *lunch box love notes* from Monday through Friday. Draft them here, and then send the actual notes to your child.

_____

_____

_____

_____

_____

_____

_____

_____

_____

_____

_____

_____

_____

_____

_____

_____

_____

_____

You know what you have to do. You go, girl!

CHAPTER 2:

Life Lessons

TAKE THIS JOURNEY WITH GUSTO, MY LOVE.

As the years go by, we collect lessons, some hard learned, some not. In the following section, you'll share lessons you believe will be useful to your loved one.

TAKE DEEP BREATHS. LET EVERYTHING
SETTLE DOWN AND GEL.

CENTER *yourself.*

LET THINGS FALL IN PLACE.

YOU ARE PREPARED. THE ANSWERS
ARE FILED IN YOUR BRAIN. YOU WILL
NEED TO CENTER YOURSELF SO THAT
YOU CAN LOCATE THEM.

Think of methods you use to **CENTER YOURSELF** when life gets too frantic. They could be physical, like deep breathing, or mental, like counting your blessings. Share these methods with your child in the space below. Add some motherly *encouragement* to remind them that **THEY CAN HANDLE ANYTHING**.

_____

_____

_____

_____

_____

_____

_____

_____

_____

_____

_____

_____

_____

_____

_____

_____

_____

_____

Good days are not always about winning the fight so much as keeping your dignity.

YOU CAN ALWAYS WIN ANOTHER DAY . . . WHEN YOU ASK YOURSELF, "WAS THAT THE VERY BEST I COULD DO?" AND YOUR ANSWER IS "FOR THAT TIME, THAT DAY, I DID MY VERY BEST," THAT'S A WIN, BABY.

That's a win!!

DESCRIBE THREE WAYS you've seen your loved one win recently. They might be obvious wins, like job promotions or great grades, or they could be subtle, such as handling a tough situation wisely.

1. _____

_____

_____

_____

_____

_____

2. _____

_____

_____

_____

_____

_____

3. _____

_____

_____

_____

_____

_____

You need to
let things go and
MOVE ON.
Otherwise, you will
stay stuck on the
ground and you will
NEVER FLY.

When have you *struggled* to let go? Tell your loved one how you managed to do it and how MOVING ON impacted your life.

_____

_____

_____

_____

_____

_____

_____

_____

_____

_____

_____

_____

_____

_____

_____

_____

_____

_____

_____

_____

_____

TIMING IS EVERYTHING,

and then there's LUCK!

Describe some of the ways you *invite luck* into your life. They might be funny rituals or quiet meditations to get into a POSITIVE MINDSET. If you have a lucky charm, include a drawing or photo of it.

_____

_____

_____

_____

_____

_____

_____

_____

_____

_____

_____

_____

_____

_____

_____

_____

_____

_____

_____

DON'T
downplay
WHAT YOU
HAVE DONE,
OR YOUR
skill.

Imagine your child is applying for their dream job. What ACHIEVEMENTS should they work into their interview? If you were writing their cover letter, what **SKILLS** would you highlight?

_____

_____

_____

_____

_____

_____

_____

_____

_____

_____

_____

_____

_____

_____

_____

_____

_____

_____

_____

_____

CHAPTER 3:

Take Care of Yourself

LET YOUR MIND SEE BEAUTY.

Be free.

LET YOUR MIND RELAX.

So many things demand our time that it's easy to forget to take care of ourselves. In this section, you can remind your child to slow down and rest. Think of what you'd say if you could whisper in their ear on a busy day. You never know which words of advice will take root.

Get in clean pj's.
Have a cup
of tea with lemon
and honey.

Simple things can have a **HUGE IMPACT** on how we feel. Think of FIVE SELF-CARE STEPS you hope your child will take on a regular basis. Make an agreement to do the same, and check in with each other to see how you are both feeling.

1. _____
_____
_____

2. _____
_____
_____

3. _____
_____
_____

4. _____
_____
_____

5. _____
_____
_____

A real friend is
one who could
tell you many
things—
but doesn't.

WHO are your real friends, and how do you make time with them a priority? List *five qualities* you hope your child will find in a GOOD FRIEND.

1. _____
_____
_____

2. _____
_____
_____

3. _____
_____
_____

4. _____
_____
_____

5. _____
_____
_____
_____

You ought to
have a little
fun in life.

OTHERWISE EVERY
DAY IS LIKE GOING
TO THE DENTIST.

When your child was younger, what did the two of you do to *have fun together?* List a FAVORITE SHARED ACTIVITY and a favorite memory to go with it.

_____

_____

_____

_____

_____

_____

_____

_____

_____

_____

_____

_____

_____

_____

_____

_____

_____

_____

_____

Take a walk

WITH YOUR BEST FRIEND.

Take another walk

WITH YOUR BEST FRIEND.

Pets bring *joy*, *laughter*, and *unconditional love*. List three ways your child can spend quality time with their pet.

1. _____
_____
_____
_____
_____
_____

2. _____
_____
_____
_____
_____
_____

3. _____
_____
_____
_____
_____
_____

Relax and
stay warm!

Some of the BEST ADVICE is the simple stuff. What are some *"mom-isms"* you tell your kiddo on a regular basis? Record them here.

_____

_____

_____

_____

_____

_____

_____

_____

_____

_____

_____

_____

_____

_____

_____

_____

_____

_____

_____

_____

_____

CHAPTER 4:

Encouragement for Rainy Days

REMEMBER:

Life is falling; living is getting up—and

CHARGING

forward even when you don't want to.

As mothers, we'd all like to shield our children from hard times, but it just isn't possible. Use the prompts in this section to tell your child about times you've had to dig deep. Remind them they have what it takes to make it through.

I know you are disappointed.
It is not always the best that are
called or chosen. You thought that
being good alone would do it.
Sometimes. Mostly not. You have come
very far on your own ... Check out
the street while you are walking—

**THERE MIGHT BE
OTHER OPPORTUNITIES
YOU LIKE BETTER.**

Describe a DISAPPOINTING SITUATION that you turned into something *positive*.
Remind your child of a time you've seen them do the same.

_____

_____

_____

_____

_____

_____

_____

_____

_____

_____

_____

_____

_____

_____

_____

_____

_____

_____

_____

DO NOT LET A

challenge

BECOME AN
EXCUSE FOR

*not doing
something.*

CHALLENGING TIMES are not always negative. Often, they remind us to tap into our *inner resilience*—something often overlooked. In the space provided, tell your child why you know they are PREPARED for a current or upcoming challenge.

_____

_____

_____

_____

_____

_____

_____

_____

_____

_____

_____

_____

_____

_____

_____

_____

_____

You are prepared.
You know what you
have to do. Do it
with confidence
and honesty.

Asking for help is important, but so is establishing a good sense of *self-reliance*. Think about ways you bolster your confidence. Is there a song that helps you tap into your inner strength? A quote or verse that makes you feel like you can take on the world? Share these with your loved one and ADD ENCOURAGEMENT of your own.

_____

_____

_____

_____

_____

_____

_____

_____

_____

_____

_____

_____

_____

_____

_____

_____

We cannot lose our faith in doing the

RIGHT THING.

We are out there.

BEING PEOPLE OF CHARACTER IS IMPORTANT!

Name three ways you try to live as a *person of character* and three ways you've seen your loved one demonstrate LIVING WITH CHARACTER.

1. _____
_____
_____
_____

2. _____
_____
_____
_____

3. _____
_____
_____
_____

1. _____
_____
_____
_____

2. _____
_____
_____
_____

3. _____
_____
_____

Ownership

OF WHAT WE DO WRONG
IS AS IMPORTANT AS
TAKING OWNERSHIP OF
WHAT WE DO RIGHT.

We don't always win the trophy.

Sometimes we TRY OUR HARDEST and still *miss the mark*. When that happens, what do you try to remember? What do you hope your child will remember?

_____

_____

_____

_____

_____

_____

_____

_____

_____

_____

_____

_____

_____

_____

_____

_____

_____

_____

CHAPTER 5:

Words from the Heart

I love you.

DEAR _____,

NEVER DOUBT THAT YOU ARE LOVED.

Use the pages in this section to share your love for your child.

YOU ARE DOING JUST

fine.

BE PROUD OF WHO AND WHAT YOU ARE.

Write four sentences describing WHO YOUR CHILD IS and why they should be *proud* of themselves.

1. _____
_____
_____
_____
_____

2. _____
_____
_____
_____
_____

3. _____
_____
_____
_____
_____

4. _____
_____
_____
_____
_____
_____

You have true grit. I am very proud of you. You keep moving and walking through whatever pops up.

Give a detailed example of when your child showed TRUE GRIT. Describe what it felt like from your vantage point and how you imagine your child felt.

_____

_____

_____

_____

_____

_____

_____

_____

_____

_____

_____

_____

_____

_____

_____

_____

_____

_____

_____

_____

_____

_____

So far on your journey,
I have seen you grow and become
a woman of substance.

I AM SO PROUD OF
WHO YOU ARE.

I'M SO PROUD OF . . . (Fill in this space with all the ways your child makes you *burst* with pride).

_____

_____

_____

_____

_____

_____

_____

_____

_____

_____

_____

_____

_____

_____

_____

_____

_____

_____

_____

_____

_____

Never let
YESTERDAY
use up
too much of
TODAY.

It is important to LEARN FROM THE PAST, but it is also important to *continue moving forward*. What are some strategies you use for putting TOUGH DAYS behind you that your child might find helpful too?

_____

_____

_____

_____

_____

_____

_____

_____

_____

_____

_____

_____

_____

_____

_____

_____

_____

_____

_____

LIFE WILL BRING
MANY ADVENTURES—
GOOD AND BAD—AND
DISAPPOINTMENTS.
YOU ARE *SPECIAL*. TAKE
ALL THAT LIFE HAS TO
OFFER AND MAKE YOUR
TAPESTRY FULL AND
RICH WITH ALL THE
COLORS THAT YOU WILL
GATHER. (SOME WILL
BE DARK COLORS—BUT
THAT WILL MAKE YOUR
TAPESTRY RICHER.)

Describe a time when something unexpected turned out to be a *really great memory*. What are some of the tapestry threads that LED TO THAT MOMENT?

EVERY DAY IS A NEW CANVAS — PAINT IT THE WAY YOU WANT.

One of the reasons New Year's Day is so special is because it offers a *fresh start*. But the reality is we can make a FRESH START EVERY DAY. What are your top three tips for making a fresh start?

1. _____

_____

_____

_____

_____

_____

2. _____

_____

_____

_____

_____

_____

3. _____

_____

_____

_____

_____

_____

YOU DON'T HAVE TO KNOW ALL THE ANSWERS, BECAUSE YOU WON'T BE ASKED ALL THE QUESTIONS.

No one can know all the answers *all the time*. How do you RESPOND to situations where you don't have the answers? How do you hope your child will respond?

_____

_____

_____

_____

_____

_____

_____

_____

_____

_____

_____

_____

_____

_____

_____

_____

_____

_____

ALWAYS DO
AND BE THE

best

THAT YOU CAN. IN
OTHER WORDS, BE

you.

What are THREE THINGS you hope your child will *always* do? List them here.

1. _____

_____

_____

_____

_____

2. _____

_____

_____

_____

_____

_____

3. _____

_____

_____

_____

_____

_____

SAW THIS TODAY:

"Be someone who makes you happy."

GOOD ADVICE.

A good *quote* or piece of *advice* can stay with your child for the rest of their life. Write down one of your FAVORITE QUOTES and why it is meaningful to you.

_____

_____

_____

_____

_____

_____

_____

_____

_____

_____

_____

_____

_____

_____

_____

_____

_____

_____

_____

_____

You can make this work. This is just a challenge. It's things like this that build your skill sets.

When you think about your child's current circumstances, what SKILLS do you see your child *developing* from them? Record them here.

_____

_____

_____

_____

_____

_____

_____

_____

_____

_____

_____

_____

_____

_____

_____

_____

_____

_____

_____

_____

_____

DO YOUR THING, MY DEAR.

Take some deep breaths and just move forward.

LOVE U.

Describe a time your child has STAYED TRUE TO THEMSELVES and *found joy*.
Share a memory of your own experience doing your own thing.

_____

_____

_____

_____

_____

_____

_____

_____

_____

_____

_____

_____

_____

_____

_____

_____

_____

_____

_____

_____

POW!

MEET THE DAY
WITH GUSTO!

How do you energize yourself to GREET the day? Think of three *morning routines* your child can embrace to JUMP-START the day and list them here.

_____

_____

_____

_____

_____

_____

_____

_____

_____

_____

_____

_____

_____

_____

_____

_____

_____

_____

_____

NEVER LET ANYBODY TELL YOU THAT YOU *can't.*

A POSITIVE MINDSET can help turn any obstacle into an *opportunity*. Remind your child of a time they accomplished something they didn't think they could do.

_____

_____

_____

_____

_____

_____

_____

_____

_____

_____

_____

_____

_____

_____

_____

_____

_____

_____

_____

_____

_____

_____

REMEMBER ONE OF
COACH WOODEN'S
PRINCIPLES OF LIFE:

LIVE EACH DAY AS IF IT WERE YOUR

masterpiece.

What are some things you and your child can do to help you *treasure* each day?

_____

_____

_____

_____

_____

_____

_____

_____

_____

_____

_____

_____

_____

_____

_____

_____

_____

_____

_____

_____

_____

Don't be scared.

Scared will not allow you to move forward.

Think of a time when you've had to BE BRAVE and *share that memory* with your child. Ask them to share their own memory of a time they've been brave.

_____

_____

_____

_____

_____

_____

_____

_____

_____

_____

_____

_____

_____

_____

_____

_____

_____

_____

_____

_____

_____

Keep the faith, kid. God will lead you and take care of you. Of course, he expects you to work for it.

What helps you *keep the faith* when things are UNCERTAIN? What advice can you give your child to keep the faith?

_____

_____

_____

_____

_____

_____

_____

_____

_____

_____

_____

_____

_____

_____

_____

_____

_____

_____

_____

_____

Make this
the best day
ever!

What are some ways you can help your child have a GREAT DAY? Send them a note? Surprise them with their favorite treat? Write down two surefire ways to give your child's day a *boost*.

1. _____
_____
_____
_____
_____
_____
_____
_____
_____

2. _____
_____
_____
_____
_____
_____
_____
_____
_____

Take time to dream—
hitch your soul to
the
stars.

The following pages are free space where you can craft *personal love notes*, share FAVORITE QUOTES, or place *favorite pictures*. Use them in whatever way you'd like.

_____

_____

_____

_____

_____

_____

_____

_____

_____

_____

_____

_____

_____

_____

_____

_____

_____

_____

_____

_____

_____

ABOUT THE AUTHOR

Tell your child a little about yourself. What are your current HOBBIES OR GOALS? What is your *favorite way to spend a weekend?* Where do you hope to travel? When did you start writing in this journal, and when did you complete it?

_____
_____
_____
_____
_____
_____
_____
_____
_____
_____
_____
_____
_____
_____
_____
_____
_____
_____
_____
_____
_____

CPSIA information can be obtained
at www.ICGtesting.com
Printed in the USA
LVHW070342061121
702395LV00009B/5

* 9 7 8 1 7 3 3 8 6 5 7 5 3 *